Google

from

A to Z

From the **Shake Up Learning®** Series

Google from A to Z
©2020 by Kasey Bell

> This book is available at special discounts when purchased in quantity for use as premiums, promotions, fundraisers, or for educational purposes. For inquiries and details, go to shakeuplearningbooks.com to purchase.

Published by Shake Up Learning
Celina, TX
ShakeUpLearning.com

Cover Design by Genesis Kohler
Editing and Interior Design by My Writers' Connection

Library of Congress Control Number: On file
Paperback ISBN: 978-1-7356018-0-9
Ebook ISBN: 978-1-7356018-1-6

New Book by Kasey Bell

Blended Learning with Google
Your Guide to Dynamic Learning with Google Tools

With collaborative tools such as Google that are available 24/7, learning can take place anytime, anywhere. Traditional learning is over! Today's technology allows you to transform education and offer your students dynamic learning experiences. **In her new book, *Blended Learning with Google*, Kasey Bell teaches you how to apply her Dynamic Learning Framework with Google tools.**

Whether you are teaching in a blended environment, remotely, or somewhere in between, Kasey's latest book will empower you to use digital tools to engage your students on a deeper level. You'll explore ways to go beyond traditional learning using Google tools, get lesson ideas and ready-to-use templates, and find a Google Toolkit that will make implementation easy!

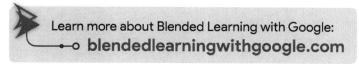

Learn more about Blended Learning with Google:
blendedlearningwithgoogle.com

Get Kasey Bell's Bestselling Book

Shake Up Learning

*Practical Ideas to Move Learning
from Static to Dynamic*

"This is the book for educators wanting to transform their classrooms and schools into dynamic hubs of learning and curiosity. I was hooked from page one, and it was so captivating that I could not put the book down! Kasey creates a compelling mix of both personal and inspirational stories to motivate and inspire every educator. She makes it easy to see how we can use technology to create dynamic learning experiences for our kids that break the mold and allow us to enter into a new frontier of learning. This book offers a great synergy of the why and how and has something in it for every teacher. Don't miss your chance to learn from one of the best in this educational page-turner!"

—Holly Clark, coauthor of *The Google Infused Classroom*

"Kasey Bell puts her finger on the pulse of education in *Shake Up Learning*. The dynamic learning framework she outlines in the book describes the kind of meaningful, authentic learning that students are craving. With discussion questions, a companion website, and room to reflect, this book is packed with resources!"

—Matt Miller, speaker, blogger, and author
of *Ditch That Textbook*

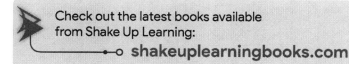
Check out the latest books available
from Shake Up Learning:
shakeuplearningbooks.com

Google Resources from ShakeUpLearning.com

The award-winning Shake Up Learning website and blog provides teachers with practical resources for using technology in the classroom. You'll find tips and strategies on how to use Google Classroom, Google for Education, and other Google tools. In addition, ShakeUpLearning.com offers many other blended learning and technology integration resources.

Find technology tips and tricks, free downloads and templates, in-depth online courses, books, lesson plans, lesson ideas, cheat sheets, blog publications, and podcasts.

Access free Google resources, tips, and downloads: **shakeuplearning.com/google**

Free Google Classroom Resources:
shakeuplearning.com/googleclassroom

Subscribe and Get a Freebie:
shakeuplearning.com/subscribe

Need Google Training for Your Entire School?

Look no further! Shake Up Learning offers a variety of programs to help your teachers learn how to meaningfully integrate Google tools and the entire suite in the classroom. From online courses to books to face-to-face training, we've got you covered!

COVID-19 forced many teachers and schools to scramble to find tools to deliver online assignments and design digital learning experiences. Google was the number one suite of tools to help make this a reality!

Shake Up Learning empowers educators, students, and parents with just-in-time resources and learning to keep learning relevant and meaningful—even during quarantine. When students return to school, Google skills will help set the foundation for more dynamic learning in the classroom.

Get your entire campus or district on board with Google! Help your teachers learn more about Google tools, Google Classroom, and meaningful technology integration strategies. You can even help your teachers become Google Certified Educators!

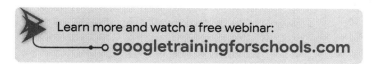

Learn more and watch a free webinar:
googletrainingforschools.com

Why Google?

We simply can't afford to ignore the power and possibility that technology—all technology, but specifically Google tools—brings to education. These days, "Going Google" is a no-brainer. Google for Education is free, readily accessible from any device 24/7, and offers an array of tools that support teaching and learning. I don't work for Google. Google doesn't pay me to promote their products. I support what I believe in, and I am excited to share strategies that will empower you to teach—and help your students learn!

If your school has "Gone Google," then chances are you are aware of some of the most popular productivity tools, such as Docs, Slides, and Gmail. But Google offers so much more! There are so many fun and engaging tools that you may not know about, and no matter what digital devices you use to support teaching and learning, you will find valuable tools to add to your teacher toolbox in this book.

What Is the Google Glossary?

I compiled this Google Glossary to help teachers build awareness and understanding of Google tools. In my new book, *Blended Learning with Google: Your Guide to Dynamic Teaching and Learning*, I will share specific lesson ideas to help teachers create dynamic learning experiences with Google tools. This supplement will help teachers build awareness, vocabulary, and their digital toolbox, and it works in conjunction with the Shake Up Learning books and online courses.

In the meantime, check out all of the free lesson ideas and tips on ShakeUpLearning.com, *The Shake Up Learning Show Podcast*, and my online courses to help you take your Google skills to the next level. A great starting point is the *Dynamic Learning with Google* podcast series and free toolkit: shakeup.link/dygoo.

Before we dive into the tools, it's important to mention that The Children's Online Privacy Protection Act of 1998 (COPPA) and The Children's Internet Protection Act (CIPA), as well as other governing laws in your state and country, may affect who can access. Some of the apps listed are restricted to those who are thirteen years old or older. Because this requirement changes as apps are updated, please be sure to comply with the terms of service and all of the applicable laws and policies when using any digital tools with your students.

What follows is an extensive (but not exhaustive) list of products and tools developed by Google. Google makes updates, additions, and changes daily, but I have included the tools and programs that I believe are most relevant to educators. So let's get started building your Google toolbox!

A

Add Ons

Add Ons are customized features that you can add to Google productivity tools such as Gmail, Google Forms, Google Sheets, Google Docs, or Google Slides. Add Ons also give you the ability to connect to third-party services outside of Google such as Pear Deck, and other favorite third-party tools.

→ developers.google.com/gsuite/add-ons/overview

A Google a Day

A Google a Day is an online game that requires students to answer a question or solve a problem by using Google Search. The game helps students better understand search strategies and key terms.

→ agoogleaday.com

AI Experiments

AI Experiments is a collection of experimental tools that use artificial intelligence. These "experiments" make it easier for anyone to start exploring machine learning through pictures, drawings, language, music, and more. This collection includes many engaging tools for students and teachers such as Quick Draw, Auto Draw, Talk to Books, and Emoji Scavenger Hunt. Keep in mind that experiments may have glitches and come and go quite often.

→ experiments.withgoogle.com/collection/ai

Alerts

Google Alerts helps you to monitor the web for interesting content. Set up a Google Alert for the topics that interest you, and you will receive alerts via email when new content is found or published online. Google Alerts are great for student research and current event projects.

→ google.com/alerts

Android

Android is Google's mobile operating system for smartphones and tablets.

→ android.com

Applied Digital Skills

Applied Digital Skills is a online, project-based learning curriculum with free lessons for teachers and students.

→ applieddigitalskills.withgoogle.com

Arts & Culture

Google Arts and Culture features content from leading museums and archives. This program makes the world's culture, history, and artifacts accessible to everyone. The wealth of knowledge and resources provide valuable insight and information to support student learning.

→ artsandculture.google.com

Assignments

Google Assignments provides a way for educators to create, analyze, and grade student work. Not to be confused with Google Classroom, this stand-alone tool also helps teachers give feedback, create a comment bank, and assign rubrics.

→ edu.google.com/assignments

B

Be Internet Awesome

Be Internet Awesome is a Digital Citizenship program for students that includes the Interland game, full curriculum, and other resources for educators.

→ beinternetawesome.withgoogle.com

Books

Google Books is a search engine that examines the full text of books, magazines, and journals. Students and teachers can use it to browse books online, find references, read reviews and suggestions, and purchase books. Google Books is great for students to explore related text and conduct research.

→ books.google.com

Blogger

Blogger is Google's free, native blogging tool. It is simple and easy to use and allows for multi-user entries. Blogger is a great platform for teacher blogs, secondary student blogs, and online portfolios.

→ blogger.com

C

Cardboard

Google Cardboard is a virtual reality (VR) headset created out of cardboard. Designed to hold a smart phone, it makes VR affordable and accessible to the masses and classrooms across the globe. VR view kits are available for purchase from hundreds of sources, or you can build your own.

→ arvr.google.com/cardboard

Calendar

Google Calendar is a calendar creation and time-management tool. Use it to create and share calendars and events, invite people to meetings, get appointment reminders, and more.

→ google.com/calendar

Certified Coach

The Google Certified Coach program empowers instructional coaches to work 1:1 with educators and drive impactful technology use in their schools. Coaches get access to research-backed strategies and tools so that new and veteran educators alike can transform instruction across every classroom.

→ edu.google.com/teacher-center/programs/certified-coach

Certified Educator

The Google Certified Educator program is a designated certification for educators and classroom teachers to demonstrate their technology integration skills and proficiency with Google tools.

——————————————→ edu.google.com/teacher-center/programs

There are two levels:

- **Level 1 Google Certified Educator** status indicates that an educator is able to successfully implement Google for Education into their teaching practice to enhance teaching and learning.

——————————→ Shakeuplearning.com/level1resources

- **Level 2 Google Certified Educator** status indicates that an educator is able to integrate a wider range of Google for Education tools and other technologies to transform their teaching practice.

——————————→ shakeuplearning.com/level2resources

Certified Trainer

The Google for Education Certified Trainer program is designed for educators with a strong history of providing Google training in schools, including creating informative learning materials and sharing enthusiasm for digital learning and technology.

——————————→ shakeuplearning.com/trainerresources

Certified Innovator

The Google for Education Certified Innovator Program supports educators in developing new projects for their classrooms and school districts. Members participate in a year-long mentorship program that begins with workshops called Innovator Academies, where teachers, coaches, and Google experts learn from each other.

→ edu.google.com/teacher-center/programs/
certified-innovator

Chat

Google Chat, formerly Hangouts Chat, is a powerful, web-based chat platform. From direct messages to group conversations, Chat allows teams to collaborate easily and efficiently. With dedicated virtual rooms and threaded conversations, it's easy to communicate with your team, department, campus, or even with students.

→ chat.google.com/welcome

Chrome

Google Chrome is Google's free, cross-platform browser. It syncs with your Google account across devices. Chrome works on any operating system, and on all your devices. Switch between your laptop, tablet, and phone, and customize Chrome to fit the needs of teachers and students with extensions, themes, and custom settings.

→ google.com/chrome

Chrome Apps

Chrome Apps are shortcuts to web applications, typically used on Chromebooks.

→ chrome.google.com/webstore/category/apps

Chrome Experiments

Chrome Experiments is a showcase of work by coders who are pushing the boundaries of web technology to create beautiful, unique web experiences inside the Chrome browser. There are lots of fun Chrome experiments that may interest teachers and students, such as Song Maker and Shared Piano.

→ experiments.withgoogle.com/collection/chrome

Chrome Extensions

Chrome Extensions are plugins for the Chrome browser that give you added features in Google Chrome, allowing the user to customize their experience.

→ chrome.google.com/webstore/category/extensions

Chrome OS

The Chrome operating system is built on the Chrome browser, where users access web apps.

→ google.com/chromebook/chrome-os

Chrome Web Store

The Chrome Web Store is where you can search for and install Chrome apps (Chromebooks only), Chrome extensions, and Chrome themes.

→ chrome.google.com/webstore

Chromebook

Powered by Chrome OS, Chromebooks are web-based laptops or tablets designed to perform most functions through the Chrome browser, and data are saved to the cloud.

→ google.com/chromebook

Chromebook App Hub

The Chromebook App Hub is an online resource to help educators, administrators, and developers work together to learn about Chromebook apps and activity ideas for schools. The App Hub is designed to bring transparency to developers' data and accessibility policies. It's also a place where school leaders can discover and learn about apps to meet the unique learning goals and policies of their school districts.

→ chromebookapphub.withgoogle.com/ideas

Classroom

Google Classroom is a free application designed to help students and teachers communicate, collaborate, and stay organized in one central hub. Educators can create classes, distribute assignments, send feedback, and see everything in one place. Classroom also seamlessly integrates with other Google tools, such as Google Docs and Drive.

→ classroom.google.com

Code with Google

All of Google's computer science programs are brought together on this page. Here you will find CS First resources, training, and curriculum, as well as other coding resources for teachers and students.

→ edu.google.com/code-with-google

Contacts

Google Contacts is a web-based application for storing and managing contact information and email addresses.

→ contacts.google.com

D

Docs

Google Docs is a free, cloud-based word processor that allows you to create, edit, and collaborate with other users in real time. All files are stored in Google Drive.

→ docs.google.com

Doodle for Google

Doodle for Google is an annual contest for K–12 students. Students are invited to create their own version of the Google logo. Winners are featured on Google.com as well as awarded scholarships and technology for their schools.

→ google.com/doodles

Drive

Google Drive is a free, cloud-based storage service that enables users to store and access files online. The service syncs stored documents, both Google file types, including Docs and Slides, and other files across all of the user's devices, including mobile devices, tablets, and personal computers.

→ drive.google.com

Drawings

Google Drawings is a free, cloud-based image creation application that allows users to collaborate and work together in real time to create images, infographics, flowcharts, organizational charts, mind maps, concept maps, timelines, and other types of images. All files are stored in Google Drive.

→ drawings.google.com

E

Earth

Google Earth is the world's most detailed globe. Use it to explore the world in high definition, tell stories, and create journeys. Google Earth allows you to draw on the map, add your own photos and videos, and customize the view, as well as share and collaborate.

→ google.com/earth

- **Google Earth for Chrome** works in the browser on desktops, laptops, and Chromebooks.
- **Google Earth for mobile** browse the globe on your phone or tablet. (Available on iOS and Android)
- **Google Earth Pro** is a desktop application that can be downloaded for free. It offers advanced features and allows users to import and export GIS data, and explore historical imagery.

→ google.com/earth/versions

Earth Engine

Google Earth Engine combines a catalog of satellite imagery and geospatial datasets with planetary-scale analysis capabilities. Scientists, researchers, developers, and educators can use this resource to detect changes, map trends, and quantify differences on the Earth's surface.

→ earthengine.google.com

Earth Studio

Earth Studio is an animation tool for Google Earth's satellite and 3D imagery. Earth Studio works with the desktop version of Google Chrome.

→ google.com/earth/studio

Earth VR

Explore Google Earth in virtual reality! Using the power of Google Earth in VR, you and your students can stroll the streets of big cities, soar over landmarks, and explore the world, all without leaving the classroom.

→ arvr.google.com/earth

Expeditions

Google Expeditions is a 360-degree VR and augmented reality (AR) app that allows teachers and students to explore the world through virtual tours. Through ready-made lessons, students can climb a mountain, hike the desert, swim with sharks, visit outer space, and more, without leaving the classroom.

→ edu.google.com/products/vr-ar/expeditions

Experiments with Google

Coders have created thousands of amazing experiments using Chrome, Android, AI, Web VR, AR, and more. Experiments are showcased on this site, along with helpful tools and resources, to inspire others to create new experiments. Use experiments to engage and inspire creativity.

→ experiments.withgoogle.com

F

Forms

Google Forms is a cloud-based survey and quiz tool. Teachers can use it to assess, collect and analyze data, and even create self-graded quizzes. All files are stored in Google Drive.

→ docs.google.com/forms

G

Gmail

Gmail is Google's free, web-based email service, and is a part of Google for Education, giving users an ad-free email experience.

→ gmail.com

Groups

Google Groups makes it easy for groups of people—such as teams, departments, or classmates—to communicate and collaborate. You can send an email to everyone in a group with one address, invite a group to an event, or share documents with a group. You can also create a discussion board or a question and answer board. Google Groups are great for online, threaded discussions.

→ groups.google.com

Google for Education

Google for Education is a powerful suite of Google tools and services that are tailored for schools. It is available globally to all educational institutions that qualify. Google for Education can help you increase opportunities for critical thinking, communication, collaboration, and creativity, all while supporting the learning objectives that you have for your students. Accessible 24/7, from just about any device, students and teachers can use one login to access all their files and tools.

→ edu.google.com

H

Help

Also known as the Google Support Center, Google Help is a great place to find support for Google products, answers to frequently asked questions, and how-to steps.

→ support.google.com

Home/Nest Devices

Google Home and Google Nest devices are smart home devices designed to make life easier by helping you do things like play music, set timers, check the weather, manage your tasks, and plan your day—using only your voice.

→ store.google.com/category/connected_home

I

Images

Google Images is a visual search engine for finding photos and illustrations on the web.

→ images.google.com

Interland

Interland is a free, web-based digital citizenship game for students. Interland is part of Google's Be Internet Awesome Digital Citizenship program and curriculum.

→ beinternetawesome.withgoogle.com/en_us/interland

J

Jamboard

The Jamboard device (hardware) is an interactive whiteboard touchscreen display used for collaboration and bringing ideas together.

→ cloud.withgoogle.com/hardware

Jamboard is also a stand-alone cloud-based application (software) that can be used for collaboration across multiple devices. Students can use this application to collaborate, create presentations, and bring together resources from other Google apps and the web.

→ jamboard.google.com

K

Keep

Google Keep is a cloud-based note-taking application and to-do list manager. Users can create and share notes and lists, add images, voice, and other media, and access across multiple devices. Keep is a great tool for teachers to manage their long to-do lists, and for secondary-grade students to take ownership of their project assignments and timelines.

→ keep.google.com

M

Maps

Google Maps is a cloud-based mapping service that allows you to search the world for cities, addresses, or businesses, and get directions. You can also use it to access Streetview and 3D imagery, share directions and locations with others, and access local information. Maps is another great application for students to explore the world around them, both locally and abroad.

→ google.com/maps

My Maps

Google My Maps is a custom map tool that allows you to create custom maps to remember your favorite places, explore new cities, plan vacations, or explain historical or fictional journeys. You and your students can create custom maps and access them from multiple devices.

→ google.com/maps/d/

Mars

Google Mars is a web-based surface map of the planet Mars. Explore different regions, mountains, plains, and craters, and search for signs of life.

→ google.com/mars

Meet

Google Meet (formerly Google Hangouts and Hangouts Meet) is a web-based video conferencing tool that allows users to video chat, host meetings, create virtual classrooms, and share their screens or presentations.

→ meet.google.com

Moon

Google Moon is a web-based surface map of Earth's moon. Tour the lunar landing sites, examine 3D models of rovers and landers, view 360-degree photo panoramas, and watch TV footage of the Apollo missions.

→ google.com/moon

N

Nest (see Google Home/Nest)

→ store.google.com/us/category/google_nest

P

Play

Google Play is the app store for Android phones and tablets, where you can search, download, and install apps.

→ play.google.com/store

Photos

Google Photos is a free, cloud-based storage location for all your photos and videos. It automatically organizes images and makes them easy to share. You can also use it edit photos and videos, and create movies, animations, and collages.

→ photos.google.com

Public Data Explorer

The Google Public Data Explorer makes large public datasets, such as the U.S. Census data, easy to explore, visualize, and communicate.

→ google.com/publicdata/directory

S

Search

Google Search is the world's largest web search engine. Search for text, keywords, phrases, documents, and more.

→ google.com

Search Education

Google Search Education is a collection of Search Literacy Lesson Plans for teachers and students, including selecting the best search terms, narrowing search results, and evaluating the credibility of sources. Each topic has lesson plans for beginner, intermediate, and advanced levels.

→ google.com/insidesearch/searcheducation

Scholar

Google Scholar provides teachers and students a simple way to search for scholarly literature. From one place, you can search across many disciplines and sources, including articles, theses, books, abstracts, and court opinions, from academic publishers, professional societies, online repositories, universities, and other websites.

→ scholar.google.com

Sheets

Google Sheets is a cloud-based spreadsheet program that allows users to create and edit files online while collaborating with other users in real time. A **spreadsheet** or worksheet is a file made of rows and columns that help sort data, arrange data easily, and calculate numerical data. Google Sheets is great at analyzing data, creating charts, and calculating. All files are stored in Google Drive.

→ docs.google.com/spreadsheets

Sky

Google Sky is like a planetarium to view space. Explore the Solar System, constellations, stars, galaxies, and nebulae.

→ google.com/sky

Slides

Google Slides is a cloud-based presentation program that allows users to create and edit files online while collaborating with other users in real time. Slides is great for teacher and student presentations, as well as a fantastic tool for interactive learning, ebooks, storytelling, and more. All files are stored in Google Drive.

→ docs.google.com/presentation

Sites

Google Sites is a cloud-based website creation tool that allows users to build, create, share, and publish for individuals, groups, schools, or the public. It integrates with other Google apps so you can easily embed other Google Drive files such as presentations. Google Sites are great for teacher websites, student projects, and e-portfolios. All files are stored in Google Drive.

→ sites.google.com/new

Street View

Street View, by Google Maps, brings a map to life, consisting of millions of panoramic and 360-degree images. Street View's content comes from Google and from outside contributors sharing their own images.

→ google.com/streetview

T

Takeout

Google Takeout is a tool that allows you to export and download your data from the Google products you use, such as your email, calendar, and photos. In a few easy steps, create an archive to keep for your records or import your data into another Google account.

→ takeout.google.com

Tasks

Google Tasks is a simple to-do list manager that integrates with Gmail and Google Calendar. You can easily turn email messages into tasks, create multiple lists, and add due dates. To access on a desktop, Chromebook, or laptop, click on the Tasks icon in the right-hand sidebar of Gmail, Calendar, Docs, Sheets, or Slides. On mobile, download the Tasks app. There is no direct link to a stand-alone Tasks app.

Teach from Anywhere

Google created this website and hub of resources and tools to support teachers and families during the coronavirus crisis and subsequent school closures. Here you will find free resources, tutorials, and support for remote teaching and learning.

→ teachfromanywhere.google

Teacher Center

Google for Education's Teacher Center is a free online platform created by educators for educators. Whether you're comfortable using technology in the classroom or just getting started, Teacher Center offers free resources and training to expand your Google skills at any level.

→ edu.google.com/teacher-center

Tips

Google Product Tips is a free resource site for tips to help anyone learn about Google products and features.

→ get.google.com/apptips/tips

Tour Creator

Tour Creator enables students and teachers to tell stories in VR. Think student-created Google Expeditions! You can create a VR tour using imagery from Google Street View or your own 360-degree photos.

———————————————————→ arvr.google.com/tourcreator

Transformation Center

Use the Google for Education Transformation Center to explore and learn from real-life examples from school leaders. You'll discover new ideas, best practices, guides, and templates.

———————————————→ edutransformationcenter.withgoogle.com

Translate

Google Translate is a free service that translates words, phrases, and webpages in more than one hundred languages.

———————————————————→ translate.google.com

Trends

Google Trends is a data tool that reveals what people are searching for on Google.com. This tool helps teachers and students analyze current and cultural events.

———————————————————→ trends.google.com/trends

V

Voice

Google Voice gives you a web-based phone number that can be used to place and receive calls from smartphones, tablets, and computers. Many teachers use Google Voice to communicate with parents and students instead of giving out their personal phone numbers.

→ voice.google.com

Voice Experiments

Google Voice Experiments is a showcase of what's possible when you bring open-ended, natural conversation into games, music, storytelling, and more. There are some fun voice experiments like Story Speaker and Mystery Animal to explore. Keep in mind that things labeled "experiment" are in a testing phase, and they often come and go.

→ experiments.withgoogle.com/collection/voice

W

Google Workspace (formerly G Suite)

Google Workspace is a suite of secure, cloud-based, productivity applications powered by Google AI, including Gmail, Docs, Drive, Calendar, Meet, and more..

→ workspace.google.com

Y

YouTube

YouTube is a video streaming and sharing service in which users can watch, like, share, and comment on videos, upload their own videos, and create their own channels. YouTube is also the world's second largest search engine. Teachers and students can learn just about anything on YouTube.

→ youtube.com

Final Thoughts

Given the nature of how quickly technology changes, this list will grow and evolve over time. The printed copy cannot keep up! *To stay informed about Google updates, new tools, and features, follow the Google Workspace Updates blog and the Keyword Blog for the latest information.*

→ Google Workspace Updates Blog: gsuiteupdates.googleblog.com

→ The Keyword Blog: blog.google

I hope you have added a few new tools and ideas to your teacher toolbox! What's next? Learn how to use these tools for meaningful learning with students. Use this book to supplement your favorite Shake Up Learning books and resources.

Don't forget to check out the other books from Shake Up Learning to get more lesson ideas, templates, and tips!

→ ShakeUpLearningbooks.com

What tools did you add to your toolbox?

Share your ideas on social media, using the

#ShakeUpLearning

hashtag, or in the Shake Up Learning community. We'd love to hear from you!

Online Courses from
Shake Up Learning

Shake Up Learning offers a variety of online, self-paced courses on many Google topics, including Google Classroom, Google Slides, and Google Certification. We also offer online workshops on dynamic learning and meaningful technology integration.

Some of our most popular courses include:

The Google Classroom Master Class

The Google Slides Master Class

The Google Certification Academies

The Dynamic Learning Workshop

Join today to take your blended learning skills to the next level!

Shake Up Learning offers free resources and webinars to help educators get Google Certified. Let Kasey be your guide on your journey to becoming a Google Certified Educator, Level 1, Level 2, or even become a Google Certified Trainer.

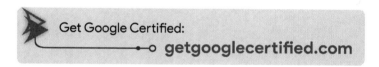

Get Google Certified:
getgooglecertified.com

Join the Community

Fans and readers of *Shake Up Learning* make up an extraordinary community of like-minded educators who are dedicated to making a difference in the lives of students. They wake up each day ready to shake up learning! As creator of *Shake Up Learning,* I wanted an online space where readers and fans could connect, find encouragement, share ideas, support one another, and discuss *Shake Up Learning* blog posts, resources, and this book.

Visit **shakeuplearning.com/community** to join the *Shake Up Learning* community of inspired educators. Here you can connect with others who are also practicing ideas to create dynamic, meaningful learning.

I look forward to seeing you there!

If you'd like to connect with me on Twitter, Instagram, or TikTok, follow **@ShakeUpLearning.**

Connect with the community on social media using the **#ShakeUpLearning** hashtag.

with Kasey Bell

◦— ShakeUpLearningShow.com —◦

The Shake Up Learning Show is a weekly podcast hosted by Kasey Bell. The show, designed for K–12 teachers and educators, features tech tips, lesson ideas, practical advice, on-air coaching, student interviews, and interviews with inspiring educators.

New episodes are released every Tuesday. You can find *The Shake Up Learning Show* on Apple Podcasts, Google Podcasts, Stitcher, Spotify, or wherever you find your favorite podcasts. You can also stream on ShakeUpLearning.com.

Bring the Power of Kasey Bell and the Shake Up Learning Message to Your School, District, or Event!

With more than thirteen years' experience as a speaker, presenter, and professional learning facilitator, and seventeen years' experience as an educator, Kasey Bell brings her unique brand of practical teaching ideas, inspiration, bold personality, and southern charm to every engagement. She has traveled the world delivering inspirational keynotes, workshops, and interactive conference presentations at world-renowned conferences, school districts, and private schools, and has even hosted her own events. Kasey has spoken at the International Society for Technology in Education (ISTE) Conference, Texas Computer Educators Association (TCEA) Convention, the Teach Tech Play Conference in Melbourne, Australia, Future of Education Technology Conference (FETC), Michigan Association for Computer Users in Learning (MACUL), and is regularly invited by Google to present to educators around the globe.

What Teachers Are Saying about Kasey Bell ...

"Kasey's trainings are ALWAYS worth it! This session was packed with ideas I could implement right away!"

—Laura Swearingen

"I was very excited to hear someone present on ideas that are important to me. I teach special education and have been 'shaking up' the learning for my students for years. I have often been criticized for my approach, and at times reprimanded. It is past time that education takes on a new approach. Thank you for being a leader and voice for change."

—Candance Baty

"Kasey Bell was amazing. I appreciated her energy, expertise, and experience. The examples, strategies, and resources she shared were so valuable and accessible for people at all levels. Thank you so much for the opportunity to hear her speak and learn from/with her. I could spend hours hearing her talk about her ideas."

—ERLC Innovation Summit in Edmonton,
Canada, participant

"If you are attending a conference, follow these steps: 1. Search by presenter. 2. Find Kasey Bell. 3. Put all her sessions on your schedule! You will learn so much and have a great time doing it!"

—Stacy Menifee

"Best session I went to at FETC. ... So much wonderful information and every bit of it useful!"

—Luanne Rowland

"Loved your session! I attended two last time you attended KySTE. Your enthusiasm is amazing and definitely encourages us to be our better selves for our students."

—Autumn Mattingly

About the Author

Kasey Bell is part sparkling smile, part witty personality, and a whole heap of passion as big as Texas. As a former middle school teacher with nearly seventeen years in education, Kasey has made it her mission to be a disruptor of the boring and to push the bounds of traditional teaching and learning.

Kasey found her true passion in digital learning. With a master's degree in educational technology and a whole bunch of crazy ideas, she migrated to the role of instructional technologist. Now, Kasey is a digital learning coach, consultant, and trainer for Shake Up Learning, based in Texas. As her passion grew, so did her need to share and connect, and Kasey started sharing her passions through her blog, ShakeUpLearning.com.

Kasey is an engaging, innovative, from-the-heart sharer who inspires educators while transforming their teaching with original, dynamic, and use-tomorrow ideas for student choice, differentiation, and technology integration. Whether creating learning from home through online courses, leading conference workshops, or presenting as a keynote speaker, Kasey is a relentless innovator of ideas and a devoted transformer of classrooms and teaching.

Through the *Shake Up Learning Show* podcast, teacher-empowering books and workshops, and the award-winning educational resources offered at ShakeUpLearning.com, Kasey proves that educators should never settle for the static and boring. When it comes to bringing out the very best in our students, we should always strive to Shake Up Learning!

Made in the USA
Las Vegas, NV
12 July 2021

26317356R00024